Syrup from Sweet Sorghum

British Library Cataloguing-in-Publication Data
A catalogue record for this book is available from the
British Library

Homemade Syrups, Vinegars and Liqueurs

It is incredibly easy to make syrups, vinegars and liqueurs at home. Essentially, the process involves steeping or cooking your chosen ingredients in liquids – waiting – straining – and then consuming! Liqueurs are perhaps the most technical of the three, with an interesting background. All that 'liqueur' means, is 'an alcoholic beverage, made from a distilled spirit that has been flavoured with fruit, cream, herbs, spices, flowers or nuts, and bottled with added sugar or other sweetener.'

Liqueurs are historical descendants of herbal medicines; they were made in Italy as early as the thirteenth century and were often prepared by monks (e.g. Chartreuse, a French liqueur made by the Carthusian Monks according to the instructions set out in a secret manuscript, given to them by François Annibal d'Estrées in 1605). Nowadays, liqueurs are made worldwide and are served in many ways: by themselves, poured over ice, with coffee, mixed with cream or other mixers to create cocktails, etc. They are often served with or after a dessert, and very frequently used in cooking. Some liqueurs are prepared by infusing certain woods, fruits, or flowers, in either water or alcohol, and adding sugar or other items, and yet others are distilled from aromatics. Anise liqueurs have the interesting property of turning from transparent to cloudy when added to water: the oil of anise remains in solution in the presence of a high concentration of alcohol, but crystallizes when the alcohol concentration is reduced; known as the ouzo effect.

Most homemade liqueurs are less complex however! Many people will use vodka as a starting spirit, because it is colourless – allowing for a wide variety of aesthetic effects, and largely flavourless, making it the ideal blank canvas on which to experiment. Cream and fruit liqueurs are the most popular (often using rum, gin, tequila and whiskey infusions as well) – and a good quality alcohol is essential. This is especially the case if you want to enjoy your creations neat. Extracts can be used, but it is always better to use the 'real' ingredients. Although this latter course will take longer (for example, steeping plums/damsons/sloes in gin for three months at least), the benefits will far outweigh the wait. Using fresh ingredients also enables the budding drinks maker to introduce more diversity, as there simply are not as many extracts as there are herbs, fruits and spices.

When it comes to creating your own unique liqueur, recipes should only be followed as the individual sees fit. Liqueur making is more of a matter of taste than an exact science, and infuses can always be diluted with additional alcohol if they taste too strong. If there is sediment left over from fruit and herb infusions, the liquid can easily be strained through a muslin cloth, and sugar syrup can be added if the mix is too tart. The end result should always be kept in a container with a tight-fitting lid, to help it keep as long as possible – and also, if possible stored in a dark place. Once the hard work is over, homemade liqueurs are fantastic served on their own, cold with ice – or when mixed into coffees, cocktails, ice-creams, desserts and any number of dishes!

Vinegars and syrups are perhaps simpler, vinegar being slightly more time consuming however. Homemade vinegar is simply achieved by mashing the fruit of your choice, straining all of the pulp from the juice, and then bottling the results for months until its ready to use. There are more possibilities to vinegar creation than one would initially expect – with a massive array of potential ingredients. The most popular form is cider vinegar (a type of vinegar made from cider or apple must, usually having a pale amber colour), which can be made by crushing the apples then straining the juice through a muslin bag. The resultant juice should, in a similar way to liqueurs, be poured into glass containers (preferably dark, or placed in a dark environment) – but with their tops covered with material, held in place with rubber bands or string. The air that is thereby allowed to get in will help the brewing process. This should take about half a year or so, but after this the vinegar will be ready to strain and bottled up.

When brewing vinegar, a substance will form on top of the liquid, and this is called 'the mother'. It can be retained and used as a starter (in a similar way to yeast) for another batch or to transform other foodstuffs, such as mead, or homemade wines into vinegars. Of course, any other ingredients apart from apples can be used – including herbs; mind, basil, tarragon or dill, or a wide selection of fruits. Have fun experimenting!

Last but not least – homemade syrups. If the reader has given any thought to liqueur or vinegar making, these will be incredibly easy. The process involves cooking any ingredient, be it spices, vanilla, caramel, peppermint, fruits, coffee...etc., with a basic syrup, consisting of one cup of sugar to one cup of water. The mix is then brought to the boil, simmered for a further 15-20 minutes and taken off the heat. Again, strained if necessary. The wonderful thing about making your own homemade products is the fun one can have with creating customised labels and garnishes to the finished bottles (think berries, citrus zest, herb sprig) – a perfect present as well as personal treat. We hope that the reader is inspired by this book to create their own liqueurs, vinegars or syrups. Enjoy.

SYRUP FROM SWEET SORGHUM

By W. V. CRUESS

In a recent publication, Hunt[1] makes the following statement: "In California, perhaps the most important single item tending to increase animal production, including dairy products, is the building of silos. This is not because there are any magical food qualities in silage, but chiefly because if a stockman or dairyman has a silo, he will raise something with which to fill it.... It is likely to be Indian corn, sweet sorghum, or Egyptian corn. The investigations at the University Farm at Davis indicate that the sweet sorghums are well adapted for silage purposes."

Woll and Voorhies[2] have found that sweet sorghum silage, per unit of dry matter furnished in the rations, proved more efficient for milk production than other forms of silage tested.

Since it is a proven fact that silage is a very important factor in animal and milk production, and since the practical feeding tests noted above have shown the superiority of sweet sorghum silage, it is probable that a considerable acreage will be planted to sweet sorghum this season. At the present time, there is a shortage of sugar. It is therefore desirable, wherever possible, to increase the production of sugar substitutes. One of the most acceptable substitutes for some purposes is sorghum syrup.[3]

If sweet sorghum is planted for silage on irrigated or sub-irrigated land, it will usually be a simple matter to plant from one to five acres more for sorghum syrup manufacture. Should conditions at the time of harvesting warrant it, this sorghum could then be used for syrup making. Otherwise, it could be used as forage.

This publication describes methods of making syrup from sweet sorghum, and more particularly, such methods as are adapted to

---

[1] Circular 187, University of California Experiment Station, Utilizing the Sorghums, by Thomas Forsyth Hunt.

[2] Bulletin 282, University of California Experiment Station, Trials with California Silage Crops for Dairy Cows, by F. W. Woll and E. C. Voorhies.

[3] The Division of Viticulture is also developing a promising method of producing syrup from cull table grapes, second-crop muscat grapes and other products of the vineyard which either go to waste or are incompletely used as food material. It appears probable that syrup from grapes can be produced at less expense for labor per unit of sugar than from sorghum.

small-scale operations. In many localities where sorghum will be grown, some one will be found who has made sorghum syrup and can direct others in operating the machinery used. Where no one with experience in syrup manufacture is available, the university will undertake to give what instruction may be needed in addition to the information contained here.

Varieties of Sorghum for Syrup.—Madson[4] has found that late sweet sorghums produce more gross weight per acre than early varieties and that the yield is in some measure proportional to the length of the growing season. Where seed can be obtained, these late high-yielding varieties will be grown for silage, in preference to the early varieties. Other things being equal, varieties producing the greatest yield of cane will also produce the greatest yield of syrup.

Of the varieties tested, Madson found that the Honey Sorghum gave the highest yield per acre, in experiments extending over three seasons at Davis. In 1915, it yielded over 30 tons per acre, and in 1914 and 1916, over twenty-six tons per acre. Other good varieties tested at Davis are Red Amber, Orange Sorghum, and Planters Sorghum. Early Amber and other early varieties gave poor yields. Orange sorghum has given good results for syrup manufacture at Riverbank, California, where it was grown commercially by L. R. Bright. Black Amber was found unsatisfactory by Mr. Bright.

Sweet Sorghum Culture.—The planting and cultivation of sweet sorghums are practically the same as for the grain sorghums, as described by Madson in Bulletin 278 of this station. If any great quantity of cane is to be made into syrup it should be planted at intervals of two weeks to insure a supply of cane over a considerable period of crushing. Dates of planting suggested are April 1, April 15, May 1, May 15, and May 30.

Sweet sorghum for syrup should be well supplied with water by irrigation or by sub-irrigation. The yield of juice will be small and the cane difficult to crush if the moisture is insufficient.

Harvesting.—The sorghum is best for syrup making from the time when the seed has reached the hard dough stage to the time of its dry stage. If the cane is cut too green, the syrup will have an unripe taste; if cut too ripe, the cane will yield a juice of inferior flavor and difficult to clarify.

The cane must be worked up within one or two days of the time it is cut. If held longer, it will become too dry, or if placed in piles to prevent drying, it will become sour through "heating" (fermentation).

---

[4] B. A. Madson, Project 283, University of California Experiment Station.

The leaves should be stripped from the cane before it is cut. This can be done by special tools made for the purpose, or a wooden "sword" made from a barrel stave will answer the purpose very well. Suckers should also be removed. · Leaves and suckers injure the flavor and render the juice difficult to clarify.

In California, the cutting of the cane will, in most cases, be done by hand. Corn binders can be used. The cane is cut six to eight inches above the ground and stacked with the heads all in the same direction.

(Courtesy of Blymer Iron Works)
Fig. 1.—Horse-power sorghum mill.

The heads must be cut from the canes. This can be done in the field and the heads thrown into piles to be collected later.

The leaves from stripping are good for forage and silage. Under normal conditions they will amount to about 200 pounds per ton of sorghum. They should be gathered as soon after stripping as possible to avoid excessive drying. The seed is a very important by-product and should amount to at least 1000 pounds per acre, worth at present prices 3c a pound or more (see p. ??). The seed can be dried and threshed as described for grain sorghum by Madson in Bulletin 278 of this station.

Crushing and Pressing the Cane.—The stripped and topped cane must be subjected to very heavy pressure to extract the juice. The usual method is by passing the cane between two or three heavy iron rollers, set at such a distance apart that the cane is crushed and most of the juice is pressed out at one operation.

There are a number of forms of sorghum mills. Some are operated by horse-power, large ones by gasoline engines, electric motors, or steam power, and very small mills may be had that are operated by hand power. For the small syrup factory the horse-power mills have sufficient capacity.

Most horse-power mills are equipped with three upright rolls, 6 to 12 inches in length and 6 to 14 inches in diameter. They are operated by a sweep attached to the top of the mill. (See figs. 1 and 2.) These mills have a capacity of from 2 to 18 tons per day. Their price varies from $25 to $320.

Fig. 2.—Horse-power mill on ranch of L. R. Bright, Riverbank. Mill is set well off ground so that juice may be received in barrels.

The engine-power mills are equipped with horizontal rolls. (See fig. 3.) Their capacity varies from 10 to 60 tons per 12 hours, and their prices from $75 to $2000 or more.

The rolls should be set at such a distance apart and the cane should be fed at such a rate that the maximum amount of juice is obtained. This can be determined by trial. For rapid feeding the rolls will be set farther apart than for slow feeding of the mill. With sorghum of average juice content, at least 100 gallons of juice should be obtained per ton of stripped cane. This figure can be used as an indication of the efficiency of the mill.

Second Pressing.—The pressed cane may be moistened with water and pressed a second time. This will yield a juice lower in sugar content and inferior in quality to the first pressing. It should be concentrated and kept separately. If a sufficient supply of cane is available, the second pressing should be omitted.

Straining the Juice.—The juice from the press is received in a tank or barrel. It should be strained through a fine screen to remove coarse particles of pulp.

(Courtesy of Blymer Iron Works)

Fig. 3.—Power sorghum mill. Electric motor or gasoline power may be used.

Settling the Juice.—Before going to the evaporating pan, the juice should be permitted to deposit as much of its sediment as possible. This fine sediment, if left in the juice, causes the latter to stick to the pan and burn. A shallow pan, such as that shown in figure 4, and

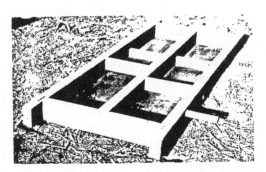

Fig. 4.—Settling trough to be placed between mill and receiving barrel.

equipped with "riffles" or transverse strips across the bottom as shown, and transverse "baffles" or strips so placed that the juice will pass beneath them, will remove a great deal of the suspended material.

6

This pan may be placed beneath the crusher. The juice flows from the crusher into the pan and as it traverses the pan the settlings are held by the bottom strips, while floating material is held by the upper strips. The settled juice flows out through the spigot at the end of the pan into a barrel or tank. This spigot is set above the bottom of the pan to avoid draining the settlings. The settling pan or trough may be made of wood and is about 4 to 6 inches deep. The one shown in the figure is about 4 feet long. It is more effective if 10 to 20 feet long and equipped with a larger number of "riffle" and "baffle" strips.

In addition to the settling device described above, several shallow tanks or vats about 2 feet deep should be provided for further settling of the juice for three or four hours before it is concentrated. The type of tank shown in figure 5 can be used for this purpose.

Fig. 5.—Settling tank for juice or syrup.

Clearing the Juice by Heating and Settling.—The juice may be made still clearer by heating it to boiling and allowing it to stand several hours after the heat is turned off. A coagulation of the albuminous matter occurs during heating. Part of this comes to the surface and can be skimmed off. Part settles and is separated by drawing off the juice above the sediment. An extra tank should be provided for this settling process. The clear juice is then ready for concentration.

The sediment and skimmings may be strained through a cloth bag until clear enough for concentration or may be mixed with the pressed cane to be used for forage or silage. This material should not be wasted.

Clearing and Neutralizing the Juice with Precipitated Chalk or Whiting.—If the juice is very sour and does not settle well after heating it may often be improved by adding precipitated chalk or a good grade of whiting (carbonate of lime) in small amounts to the boiling juice until the juice will no longer turn a piece of blue litmus paper red. The amount used will be about one half to one ounce of whiting per gallon. Only the best whiting should be used. An excess will do no harm. The treated juice is allowed to settle several hours after heating and before drawing it off from the sediment for concentration. It is usually not necessary or advisable to use whiting or chalk for small-scale operations.

Clearing by Filtering.—Where small quantities of syrup are to be made, the fresh juice may be cleared by heating to boiling followed by filtering while hot through a filter bag made of felt or heavy cloth. The process is, however, exceedingly slow and will usually not repay the effort. On a very large scale it would be possible to use a force pump and a large filter press to clear the hot juice. Another method of clearing the juice is to concentrate it to about one-half its original volume and then filter it through sand or excelsior. A shallow box 4 to 6 inches deep filled with sand may be used. Clay and milk of lime have been used for clarifying the juice, but their use is not recommended for the beginner.

Concentration of the Juice.—After most of the sediment has been removed, the juice is ready for evaporation to a syrup. This may be done in any one of several forms of evaporators described below.

1. *By Use of Iron Kettle.*—The simplest form of syrup evaporator is a cast-iron kettle heated with a wood fire. This apparatus will give a very dark colored syrup because of the long heating necessary and because the juice acts upon the iron of the kettle, forming a dark

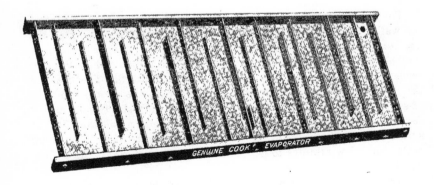

(Courtesy of Blymer Iron Works)

Fig. 6.—Continuous pan evaporator. This is the most common type of pan used.

colored compound. It should be used only where a more satisfactory evaporator can not be obtained.

2. *By Use of Continuous Pan and Portable Fire Box.*—A very satisfactory evaporating outfit for small-scale operations is shown in figures 6 and 7. The evaporating pan shown in figure 6 is made of galvanized iron or of copper. It varies in length from 5 to 15 feet. The longer pans are more satisfactory. This pan is placed over the fire box shown in figure 7. This fire box is of the same length as the pan.

(Courtesy of Blymer Iron Works)

Fig. 7.—Portable fire box for use with pan shown in preceding figure.

The fire box should be lined with fire brick or good clay to protect the walls and check radiation of heat. This must be done after the fire box is received from the manufacturer.

The clear juice is allowed to run in at the upper end of the pan from a tank or barrel placed above it as in figure 9. The fire and the flow of juice are so regulated that syrup of the proper per cent of sugar will flow from the lower end. Where very short pans (6 to 8 feet in length) are used, it is difficult to maintain a constant flow of syrup from the pan and it often becomes necessary to close the syrup outlet for a few minutes to permit the syrup to become of the desired density.

Great care must be observed in keeping the bottom of the pan covered with juice at all times to prevent scorching. During boiling, the depth of liquid in the pan should not be too great, otherwise the great length of time necessary to concentrate the juice will result in darkening. The fire should be vigorous. Light, quick-burning wood is best for use with this style of furnace. The fire should be especially hot at the stack end of the furnace where the final boiling of the syrup takes place. The more intense the fire, however, the more care must be taken to prevent scorching of the syrup. Coagulated albuminous and other materials come to the surface during boiling. These should be skimmed off. The skimmer shown in figure 8 is useful for this purpose.

(From Farmers' Bull. 477, U.S.D.A.)

Fig. 8.—Skimmer used during the concentration of the juice.

Darkening is often due to boiling the syrup to too high a sugar content; boiling should stop when the syrup has become rich enough in sugar to keep without sterilization. This point can be determined as described in the following paragraph. When the last juice has gone into the pan it should be followed with water to prevent scorching the juice that remains.

3. *Testing the Syrup.*—An experienced syrup maker can judge when the syrup has been concentrated enough, by the general appear-

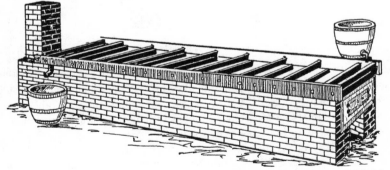

(From Farmers' Bull. 477, U.S.D.A.)

Fig. 9.—Continuous evaporator mounted on permanent brick furnace. This is the most satisfactory method of mounting the large pans.

ance and behavior of the syrup; but even his judgment is not always reliable. The point at which the boiling is sufficient can be easily and accurately determined by use of a Baumé syrup hydrometer, or a Balling hydrometer.

The hydrometer consists of a glass tube weighted at one end with shot or mercury and carrying a narrower tube or stem at the upper

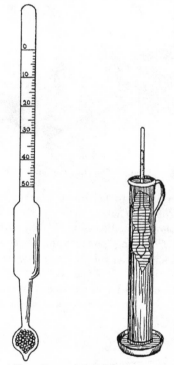

(From Farmers' Bull. 477, U.S.D.A.)

Fig. 10.—Baumé Syrup Hydrometer with Tin Cylinder to Hold Syrup for Testing.

end marked in degrees Baumé or Balling.[5] The whole instrument is about 12 inches long. A tin, copper, or glass cylinder about 1½ inches in diameter and about 12 inches in height as shown in figure 10 will be needed to hold the syrup sample.

Pour the hot syrup into the cylinder, filling it almost full. If the syrup is frothy, fill the cylinder to overflowing so that the bubbles will not interfere.

[5] Some syrup hydrometers are marked in degrees Brix. This is the same as Balling.

Insert the hydrometer into the hot syrup. Read the degree indicated on the hydrometer stem at the surface of the liquid. If the syrup is hot, that is, tested within two or three minutes from the time it is taken from the pan, it should give on the Baumé hydrometer more than 36° and less than 40°; and on the Balling or Brix hydrometer between 65° and 73°. Hot syrup gives a lower reading than the same syrup after it has cooled. For cold syrup the above figures· will be 38° to 42° Baumé and 70° to 78° Balling or Brix. These figures may be used in testing the syrup after it has cooled, in order to check the tests made during evaporation. Tests are valuable in making blends of syrup that has been concentrated too far with syrup too low in sugar content.

Syrup below 70° Balling or Brix, or below 38° Baumé (tested on cold syrup) is very apt to mold or ferment. Syrup very high in sugar may crystallize. Thirty-eight degrees Baumé in cold syrup is equivalent to 36° Baumé in hot syrup, and 70° Balling or Brix cold is equivalent to 65° in hot syrup.

4. *By Use of Continuous Pan and Permanent Furnace.*—Where long pans (12 to 15 feet) are used, they are usually mounted upon a brick furnace. Figure 9 shows such an evaporating outfit equipped for wood fuel. Under most California conditions, wood may be hard to obtain and crude oil as fuel would probably be less expensive and as satisfactory as wood. Forced feed for the oil would perhaps be necessary although the type of crude oil burner used for heating solutions used in dipping grapes for raisin making and in furnishing heat to fruit evaporators might prove satisfactory.

The pressed cane may be air-dried and used for fuel. A special large open grate is needed when this fuel is used. Companies that furnish mills and evaporators can furnish grates for this purpose, with directions for their installation and use.

The operation of this type of outfit is similar to that of the portable outfit described under section 2. A 15-foot pan can be made to produce 200 gallons of syrup per 12 hours, and a 6-foot pan 15 to 30 gallons.

5. *Steam Evaporators.*—Evaporators heated by high-pressure steam may be had. The steam evaporator consists of a long, shallow, wooden trough with a copper steam coil in the bottom. The juice enters at one end and as it flows over the coil to the lower end it is concentrated to a syrup. These evaporators produce excellent syrup of light color when properly operated. Steam evaporators will require 8 to 40 horsepower steam boilers. They are suitable for large establishments. A steam evaporator will produce 100 to 600 gallons of syrup per 12 hours, depending on its size.

6. *Vacuum Pans.*—Where a very large permanent installation is contemplated, the installation of the vacuum system of evaporation should be considered. The vacuum pan for syrup is usually an enclosed steam-heated copper kettle. Pans of commercial size vary from $1000 to $10,000 in price and will produce from 300 to 3000 gallons of syrup per 12 hours. A steam plant, vacuum pump and a large supply of water for condensation are necessary for their use.

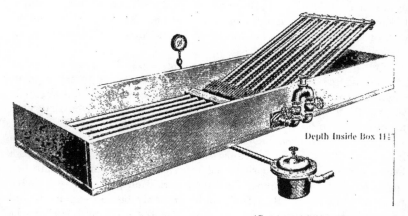

Depth Inside Box 11½

(Courtesy of Golden Foundry Co.)

Fig. 11.—A steam syrup evaporator.

Storing and Canning the Syrup.—The finished syrup may be stored in barrels. It is usually marketed in gallon or smaller cans. At the present time cans are very difficult to obtain. The syrup may also be sold in bulk in barrels or in small kegs.

OUTLINE OF PROCESS RECOMMENDED FOR THE SMALL-SCALE MANUFACTURE OF SORGHUM SYRUP

1. Equipment: Small horse-power mill; galvanized iron or copper evaporating pan 8 to 10 feet long; portable furnace for pan; settling pan about 6 to 8 feet long at crusher (see fig. 4); settling tank of about 50 gallons capacity (fig. 5); two open 50-gallon barrels for juice; receiving and settling tank for syrup, 25 gallons (fig. 5); skimmer for use during boiling of syrup; 30 or 25-gallon open barrel or wooden tub with spigot to be placed above pan for juice supply for pan (see fig. 9); several buckets and dippers.

2. Harvesting: Strip off leaves when seed is almost ripe; cut canes at 6 to 8 inches from ground. Cut off heads. Haul cane to mill at once.

3. Press as soon after cutting as possible.

4. Pass juice from the mill through settling pan below mill to settling tank.

5. Heat to boiling and allow to stand four or five hours after heat is turned off. Skim off floating material. The heating can be done in the evaporating pan and the heated juice transferred to a barrel or tank for settling.

6. Draw off settled juice as clear as possible from sediment. The sediment may be strained and used for syrup or may be used for stock feed.

7. Fill the evaporating pan with the settled juice and boil down to a syrup. Allow syrup to flow from the pan and the juice to flow into the pan at such a rate that the syrup tests when hot between 36° and 40° Baumé or between 65° and 73° Balling or Brix. (See fig. 10.)

8. Allow syrup to settle four or five hours.

9. Fill into syrup cans or kegs.

COST OF EQUIPMENT FOR SORGHUM-SYRUP MANUFACTURE
CASE A.—SMALLEST FACTORY-MADE OUTFIT

1. One small horse-power cane mill of 2–3 tons capacity per day, f.o.b. Eastern point $32.50
2. One rocker furnace, Cook's pattern, 66 inches, f.o.b. Eastern point 17.65
3. One galvanized iron Cook's pattern evaporator, 66 inches 8.80
4. Freight to any point in California (freight rate in 1914) 28.00

$86.95

In 1914 the cost of this whole outfit delivered in California was $60. The freight charge given may have increased to about $40 for this year, and if so, the cost of the entire plant would be $100.

Its capacity per day of 12 hours is about 20 gallons of syrup, or per season of 40 days, 800 gallons. This is its maximum capacity unless run longer than 12 hours a day.

CASE B.—PLANT WITH CAPACITY OF 160 GALLONS SYRUP PER 12 HOURS

1. One power cane mill with capacity of 2 tons of cane per hour; 4 h.p.....$100.00
2. One Cook evaporator, galvanized iron, 180 inches long 24.00
3. One No. 5 furnace front and grate 28 × 35 inches; door opening to furnace, 9½ × 20½ inches 14.45
4. 6Bricks (2500) and lime (3 barrels) for building furnace for evaporator, belt for motor, juice receptable above pan (100-gallon tank with spigot), syrup receiver (100-gallon tank), juice pipes, skimmer, three 20-gallon fiber tubs, ½ dozen 3-gallon fiber buckets 125.00
5. One 5-h.p. electric motor or gasoline engine 150.00
6. One hand-power pump (Woodin and Little), or similar type 25.00
7. Freight on mill, pan, and furnace door from East 50.00

$510.45

---

6 Estimate for cost of furnace from Bul. 486, U. S. Dept. Agr.

ESTIMATE OF APPROXIMATE RETURNS FROM SORGHUM SYRUP

Assumed:

1. Yield of 14 tons per acre, equal to 12 tons stripped cane.

2. Yield of 11 gallons of syrup per ton of stripped cane (or 132 gallons per acre).

3. A season of 30 working days.

4. That factory has an average capacity of 160 gallons to 170 gallons per day or about 5000 gallons for the season. This would represent about 40 acres of sorghum.

The cost of producing the syrup would be approximately as follows:

ESTIMATED COST OF PRODUCTION

The costs per acre for plowing, seeding, irrigating, cultivating, and cutting are taken from R. L. Adams, Agronomy Project 337, page 104.

	Cost per acre	Cost per ton whole cane
1. Fall plowing (Adams)	$1.75	$0.125
2. Spring plowing (Adams)	1.25	.089
3. Preparation of seed bed (Adams)	1.75	.125
4. Cost of seed (Adams)	.25	.018
5. Planting (Adams)	.30	.021
6. Cultivating and furrowing (Adams)	2.50	.178
7. Water (Adams)	1.50	.107
8. Applying water (Adams)	.75	.053
9. Cutting by hand (Adams)	1.75	.125
10. Hauling at 50c per ton (estimated)	7.00	.500
11. Stripping, topping cane and threshing and drying seed (estimated)	20.00	1.429
12. Taxes and insurance on land (Adams)	2.50	.178
13. Crushing cane and concentrating juice at factory at 18c per gallon	24.00	1.715
14. Cost of cans, shipping boxes, and labor for canning (estimate by L. R. Bright) at 25c per gallon	33.00	2.357
	$98.30	$7.020

Cost per gallon, $0.746.

VALUE OF PRODUCTS AT CURRENT PRICES

	Value per acre	Value per ton of whole cane
1. 132 gallons syrup at $1 per gallon	$132.00	$9.43
2. 1400 pounds seed at 3c lb.	42.00	3.00
3. 2500 lbs. leaves at $5 per ton	6.25	.43
4. Pressed cane (bagasse), 5 tons at $2.50, for forage	12.50	.89
Total	$192.75	$13.75

Value per gallon of syrup, $1.44.

Approximate Profit

1. Per acre, $192.75 less $98.30 .... $94.45
2. Per ton of whole cane, $13.75 less $7.02 .... 6.73
3. Per gallon of syrup, if value of by-products (seed, leaves, and cane) is deducted from cost of manufacture, $1.44 less $0.75 .... .69
4. Per gallon of syrup, excluding value of by-products, $1 less $0.75 .... .25

ESTIMATE ON BASIS OF CALIFORNIA EXPERIENCE[7]

Yield average	12	tons per acre
Yield of syrup per ton, 10 gals.	120	gallons per acre
Cost of concentrating, etc.	$0.25	per gallon
Cost of cans and boxes	.25	per gallon
Interest on plant, 10%	.01	per gallon
Cost of cultivation, irrigation, Harvesting, and stripping	.17	per gallon
Total cost	$0.68	per gallon
Total cost per acre	81.60	

Value of Products per Acre

120 gallons of syrup at $1	$120.00
1500 pounds of seed at 3c, for feed[8]	45.00
2400 pounds of leaves at $5 per ton	6.00
4 tons of pressed cane at $2.50 per ton	10.00
Total value	$181.00
Total cost	81.60
Net profit per acre	$99.40

Allowing no interest on land or rent charges.

Uses of Sorghum Syrup.—When properly made, sorghum syrup is amber in color, of about the consistency of ordinary table syrup, is usually slightly cloudy or opalescent in appearance and possesses the pleasing characteristic flavor of the sorghum cane. It is an excellent table syrup for use on hot cakes, biscuits, etc. It can also be used as a substitute for sugar in making corn bread, cup cakes, and in similar ways. When diluted with water it may be used for canning fruits for home use, or mixed with sugar in making fruit preserves. Experiments with other syrups would indicate that sorghum syrup might also be used as a sugar substitute in jelly making, if about three-quarters of a cup of the syrup is used to one cup of fruit juice.

---

[7] Figures for yield, cost of concentration, and boxes are based on estimates furnished by L. R. Bright, of Riverbank, who has made syrup on a small scale for three years. Other figures based on estimates by Adams and Madson.

[8] The present market price for sorghum seed for feeding purposes is 3¼c per pound. Sweet sorghum seed is not so satisfactory for feeding as grain sorghum seed. For seeding purposes, the price is as high as 7c to 8c per pound. Estimate of value of leaves for forage was given by Professor P. B. Kennedy and Dr. F. W. Woll.

COMPANIES FROM WHOM SORGHUM SYRUP MACHINERY CAN BE OBTAINED

1. Sears, Roebuck and Company, Chicago, Illinois (special catalogue of farm implements and machinery). Mills, open-pan evaporators, and furnaces.

2. Blymer Iron Works, Cincinnati, Ohio. Mills, open-pan evaporators and furnaces.

3. The Bahmann Iron Works Company, Cincinnati, Ohio. Mills, open evaporators and furnaces.

4. Golden's Foundry and Machine Company, Columbus, Georgia. Mills, open-pan evaporators, furnaces, and steam evaporators.

5. Berger and Carter Company, San Francisco, California. Steam evaporators, pans, mills and furnaces.

6. Cook Cane Mill and Evaporator Company, St. Louis, Missouri. Mills, open-pan evaporators and furnaces.

7. Montgomery Ward Company, Chicago, Illinois. Mills, pan evaporators and furnaces.

8. Chattanooga Plow Company, Chattanooga, Tennessee. General equipment.

9. Southern Plow Company, Columbus, Georgia. General equipment.

10. A. C. S. Bell Company, Hillsboro, Ohio. General equipment.

COMPANIES FROM WHOM SYRUP HYDROMETERS AND CYLINDERS MAY BE OBTAINED IN CALIFORNIA

1. Justinian Caire Company, San Francisco, California.
2. Braun-Knecht-Heimann Company, San Francisco, California.
3. Bausch and Lomb Company, San Francisco, California.
4. F. W. Braun Company, Los Angeles, California.

The cost of hydrometer and cylinder should not exceed $1.50. The hydrometer should be used to insure production of a syrup that will not ferment or crystallize. Syrup making should not be attempted without it. The hydrometer most easily obtained is a Baumé hydrometer with divisions from 0–50°. A glass or metal cylinder about 1½ inches in diameter and about 12 inches tall will also be needed.

It is urged that everyone seriously contemplating the manufacture of syrup during the coming season write at once to one of the above dealers and make contracts for delivery of machine. The University has been informed that there is apt to be a very great demand for this sort of equipment and that contracts should be made at once to avoid disappointment.

Printed in the USA
CPSIA information can be obtained
at www.ICGtesting.com
LVHW091005141223
766500LV00006B/220

9 781447 463931